D1648076

*This
book belongs to*

_____

*. . .a woman who delights
in God's wisdom.*

GROWTH & STUDY GUIDE

God's Wisdom
for a
Woman's Life

Elizabeth George

HARVEST HOUSE™ PUBLISHERS

EUGENE, OREGON

Cover by Terry Dugan Design, Minneapolis, Minnesota

Cover photo © Dana Edmunds, Getty Images

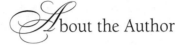

About the Author

Elizabeth George is a bestselling author and speaker whose passion is to teach the Bible in a way that changes women's lives. For information about Elizabeth's books or speaking ministry, to sign up for her mailings, or to share how God has used this book in your life, please write to Elizabeth at:

Elizabeth George
P.O. Box 2879
Belfair, WA 98528

Toll-free fax/phone: 1-800-542-4611
www.elizabethgeorge.com

GOD'S WISDOM FOR A WOMAN'S LIFE GROWTH AND STUDY GUIDE
Copyright © 2003 by Elizabeth George
Published by Harvest House Publishers
Eugene, Oregon 97402
www.harvesthousepublishers.com

ISBN 0-7369-1044-1 (pbk.)

Printed in the United States of America.

03 04 05 06 07 08 09 10 / BP-KB / 10 9 8 7 6 5 4 3 2 1

Contents

A Word of Welcome

Let me welcome you to this fun—and stretching!—growth and study guide for women who, like you, want to walk in wisdom. God has given His women timeless principles in His Word, the Bible, to help us with our every need.

A Word of Instruction

The exercises in this study guide should be easy to follow and do. And the best thing is that they center on the issues and concerns of your daily life. You'll need your copy of *God's Wisdom for a Woman's Life* and your Bible, a pen, and a heart ready to grow in wisdom. In each lesson you'll be asked to:

- Read the corresponding chapter from *God's Wisdom for a Woman's Life*.

- Answer questions designed to guide you to greater wisdom.

- Complete the personalized and practical instructions

    Just for today…
    Just for tomorrow…
    Just for this week…

A Word for Your Group

Of course, you can grow as you work your way, alone, through the biblical wisdom presented in this book and apply it to your heart. But I urge you to share the journey with other women. A group, no matter how small or large, offers personal care and adds interest. There's sharing. There are sisters-in-Christ to pray for you. There's the mutual exchange of experiences. There's accountability. And, yes, there's peer pressure—which always helps us get our lessons done! And there's sweet, sweet encouragement as together you stimulate one another to greater love, wisdom, and good works.

To aid the woman who is guided by God to lead a group, you'll find useful information in an article title "Leading a Bible Study Discussion Group" on the website www.elizabethgeorge.com.

A Word of Encouragement

No price can be put on wisdom! Indeed, "wisdom is better than rubies, and all the things one may desire cannot be compared with her" (Proverbs 8:11). The jewel of wisdom enables you and me to walk smoothly through life, encountering every need and every trial with the grace only a heart of wisdom can produce. And a woman without wisdom?—well, the Bible calls that person a fool.

If you will use the insights, tools, and how-to's gained from *God's Wisdom for a Woman's Life* and this study guide, by God's grace and armed with His timeless principles for your every need, others will begin to describe *you* as a woman of wisdom. Your wise ways will bring glory to God, your family and friends will be blessed, and your life will be enriched. (And these are just a few of the blessings wisdom reaps!) So please, come walk in wisdom. Come discover the treasure of wisdom's practical, simple, life-giving and life-changing instruction.

I Need Help with...
*W*isdom

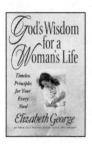

In your personal copy of *God's Wisdom for a Woman's Life* read the chapter titled "I Need Help with...Wisdom." Make notes here about what from this chapter meant the most to you or offered you the greatest challenge or helped you to grow in wisdom.

Wisdom for Your Life

As you launch into this exciting study about God's wisdom for a woman's life, take a minute to write a few sentences that describe your lifestyle and the kinds of decisions you must make on a regular basis.

Review the quotations at the beginning of this chapter in your book. Write here the one you like best and why.

The Wisdom of Solomon

Read the story about King Solomon from 1 Kings 3:4-15 in your Bible. Also read the corresponding account of Solomon's encounter with God in 2 Chronicles 1:6-13. From these accounts, in what ways do you witness Solomon's following the guidelines for wisdom taught in these scriptures?

Proverbs 4:7—

Proverbs 4:11—

Proverbs 8:11—

James 1:5—

Now for you—How are you faring in following Solomon's example of actively pursuing, desiring, and asking for wisdom? Note any weak areas. Then write out what you will do to turn up the heat of your desire to walk in wisdom.

Steps Toward Wisdom

Write out each of the four steps toward wisdom from your book and answer the questions regarding them.

Step 1—

Consider Solomon's situation again. Above what other things did he desire God's wisdom (see 1 Kings 3:11)?

Regarding long life: What did Solomon write regarding wisdom in...

...Proverbs 3:16?

...Proverbs 9:11?

Regarding wealth: What did Solomon write regarding the value of wisdom in...

...Proverbs 3:13-15?

Regarding triumph over enemies: According to Proverbs 16:7, why was seeking wisdom a good choice?

Step 2—

Again, recalling 1 Kings 3, how did Solomon model for us this step toward wisdom?

Look now at another great man and leader of God's people. How did Nehemiah also live out this most important step toward gaining wisdom in Nehemiah 1:4-6?

Step 3—
Look up and read Proverbs 2:1-6. I hope this passage soon becomes one of your favorites! What efforts must the wise person make to obtain wisdom?

And what does verse 6 have to say about where you are to seek wisdom?

Now look at Proverbs 8:17. What do you learn here about how hard you must seek for wisdom?

Revisit James 1:5. Where did James say you are to seek for wisdom?

Step 4—
As in every area of your life, you must also grow in wisdom. What are some keys to growing in wisdom according to…

...Proverbs 4:6?

...Proverbs 8:33?

...Proverbs 8:34?

Bonus blessing #1—For a glimpse at God's blessings upon King Solomon due to his request for wisdom above all other things, read 1 Kings 3:16-28 and 4:29-34. In a few words, how did God bless Solomon?

Bonus blessing #2—For an example and a glimpse of God's answer to Solomon's request for wisdom above all things, read 2 Chronicles 1:14-17. In a few words, how did God bless Solomon?

Meet Abigail—What a woman...and what a wise woman! Acquaint yourself now with her splendid wisdom by scanning 1 Samuel 25:2-39. As you read, note here in a few words how Abigail exhibited...

...wisdom

…discretion

…faithfulness

What do you most admire about Abigail that you want to take away from this lesson and make true in your life?

Just for Today

A note of instruction—I will not be guiding you through this practical and personal section on the lessons to follow, but I do want to provide you with a sample of how you can work through the suggested exercises in *God's Wisdom for a Woman's Life*. The point is, do as much as you can to apply God's wisdom to *your* life! If you are completing these lessons on your own, your answers testify to your diligence, faithfulness, and sincerity in seeking out God's wisdom. They provide a record and mark your progress as you journey toward putting God's timeless principles to work for you. If you are part of a group, write here what you will share as you are accountable to others and encourage others. And I cannot suggest strongly enough that you purchase a lovely personal journal, one that will excite you afresh each day to pick it up, put pen to paper, and log your growth. It will encourage *your* heart and add yet another discipline to your life. As Donald Whitney writes in his book on spiritual health, an example of practicing personal discipline "is in the keeping of a spiritual journal."[1]

    ❧ *Just for today*...Share how you followed through on the assignment. (For instance, *did* you follow through? What chapter of Proverbs did you read? What verse did you choose to write on your card? Did you carry it with you? Did you apply its wisdom to your heart?)

    ❧ *Just for tomorrow*...Share how you followed through on this assignment. (For instance, **did** you read a chapter from Proverbs? What decision(s) must you make? From whom did you or will you seek wise counsel?)

❧ *Just for this week*…Share how you followed through on this assignment. (For instance, what commentary on the book of Proverbs did you borrow, check-out, purchase, or put on your to-do list? Did you read along with it each day when you read your chapter of Proverbs for the day?)

Seeking a Heart of Wisdom

Please read the "Seeking a Heart of Wisdom" section in your book again. As you consider the contents of this chapter and God's wisdom for your life as a woman, what one timeless principle or truth spoke to your heart…and what do you plan to do about it?

I Need Help with...
My Priorities

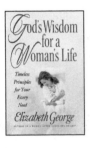

In your personal copy of *God's Wisdom for a Woman's Life* read the chapter titled "I Need Help with...My Priorities." Make notes here about what from this chapter meant the most to you or offered you the greatest challenge or helped you grow in wisdom.

As you step into this exciting lesson that focuses on a woman's priorities, think about your daily schedule and the flow of your week. Also take a look at your calendar for the past and present week. What do the facts reveal about the priorities you are living out on a daily basis? Where...and with whom...and on what... are you spending your time? Your energy? Be honest...and make notes here.

Put God First

1. This chapter began with praise for the wise woman pictured in Proverbs 31:10-31. What do you learn about her key to success in verse 30?

   What more do you learn from...

   ...Proverbs 10:27?

   ...Proverbs 14:26?

   ...Proverbs 14:27?

   ...Proverbs 19:23?

   ...Proverbs 29:25?

2. Do you realize the need for wisdom in managing your busy life? If so, where must you seek it according to...

   ...Psalm 19:7?

   ...Psalm 119:130?

3. Speaking of priorities, how does the Word of God say we can and should "begin with God"?

   Matthew 6:33—

   Matthew 22:37—

   1 Corinthians 2:1-2—

Is there anything obvious that you need to do to act upon living according to this all-important first and ultimate priority? What first step will you take today?

Serve Others

Now look at Matthew 22:39. What is our attitude toward others to be?

How did Jesus say to live this out in Matthew 20:26?

And in Matthew 20:27?

How did Jesus serve others in Matthew 20:28?

Knowing God's order of priorities—If you are married, who (and what) does God's Word say are to be the priorities in your life as found in…

…Matthew 19:5?

…1 Corinthians 7:34?

…Titus 2:4?

…Proverbs 14:1 and 31:27?

If you are not married, what does God's Word say is to be the priority of your life as stated in…

…1 Corinthians 7:34?

Take a minute to share how your initial assessment of your priorities measures up to this list. Are you on track, or do you need to make some changes? Please explain.

Planning to practice God's priorities—One of my favorite wisdom scriptures, Proverbs 16:1, centers on planning. Write out Proverbs 16:1 here.

By preparations (or plans) Solomon meant the "placing of things in order" as in "setting a battle-array" or "laying a fire."[2] God, of course, has the final say in not only your life, but in your day. But how wise and valuable it is for you to *plan* to practice God's priorities. If this week didn't look so good when you completed the exercise at the beginning of this lesson, or if it revealed the fact that your priorities are truly out of whack(!), take calendar and planner in hand and place a few things in order. Set a battle-array for next week. Turn things around by planning to practice God's priorities. Check here when done_____. Then jot down what the following proverbs add to your concept of planning and its importance.

Proverbs 16:3—

Proverbs 16:9—

Let's review—Before we move on to *self,* are you perhaps failing to serve others because of these *self*-ish habits? Check any that need your undivided and ruthless attention!

___laziness   ___sleeping in   ___lounging

___shopping   ___running around   ___telephone

___Internet   ___TV   ___hobbies

Now, thinking back to planning and "placing things in order" and "setting a battle-array," what is your *plan* for eliminating excesses in these areas so that you can better serve others? List at least three things you will do, change, or eliminate to follow God's priorities for the wise woman.

1.

2.

3.

Take Care of Yourself

Now, for yourself...and planning to practice God's priorities!—Let's follow the exercises suggested in your book:

When will you get up?

When will you go to bed?

When will you eat?

What will you eat?

When will you exercise?

What will those exercises be?

When will you take your vitamins?

What other disciplines could you use in your life?

Write out your answers, schedule them into your planner at the designated times, and pray for God's help in following through. And here's an added step—I've been encouraging you to write in a journal or keep some kind of record of your growth in wisdom. Write out the changes you experience as you put these disciplines in place. What a testimony your transformation will be to God! And just for the sake of the battle, how do these verses fortify you in the discipline of your eating habits?

Proverbs 23:2—

Proverbs 30:8—

1 Corinthians 10:31—

Galatians 5:23—

Bonus blessing—We'll continue to look at God's example of a woman of wisdom in Proverbs 31:10-31. So take a couple minutes to read through these 22 verses. Note her priorities and the disciplines that enabled her to practice them. How do you see her living out…

Priority #1—God?

Priority #2—Others?

Priority #3—Self?

Others praised her…and now it's your turn. What quality or practice do you most want to imitate from her wise life? And why?

Just for Today

❧ *Just for today…*

❧ *Just for tomorrow…*

❧ *Just for this week…*

—Seeking a Heart of Wisdom—

Please read the "Seeking a Heart of Wisdom" section in your book again. As you consider the contents of this chapter and God's wisdom for your life as a woman, what one timeless principle or truth spoke to your heart…and what do you plan to do about it?

I Need Help with...
My *P*urpose

In your personal copy of *God's Wisdom for a Woman's Life* read the chapter titled "I Need Help with...My Purpose." Make notes here about what from this chapter meant the most to you or offered you the greatest challenge or helped you grow in wisdom.

Eternal Life

Every woman needs encouragement in performing her daily tasks and duties. How do these scriptures about eternal life *encourage* you in your work today?

Psalm 16:11—

2 Corinthians 4:17—

1 Peter 1:3-4—

1 John 3:2—

Now note how you can know that you have eternal life.

John 1:12—

John 3:16—

John 6:47—

Romans 6:23—

1 John 5:11-12—

1 John 5:13—

In your book I asked you, "Do you possess the hope of eternal life?" Now it is your turn to answer that most-important question. Write a few sentences from your heart about *your* "hope of eternal life."

This Is My Prayer, Lord Jesus

- *Are you sure of eternal life?* If so, pray and thank God profusely!

- *Are you uncertain?* If so, consider the following prayers regarding your faith in God's Word and in God's Son, Jesus Christ.

Jesus, I know I am a sinner, but I want to repent of my sins and turn and follow You. I believe that You died for my sins and rose again victorious over the power of sin and death, and I want to accept You as my personal Savior. Come into my life, Lord Jesus, and help me obey You from this day forward.

Jesus, I know that in the past I asked You into my life. I thought at that time that I was Your child, but my life hasn't shown the fruit of my belief. As I again hear Your call, I want to make a real commitment to You as the Lord and Master of my life.

Jesus, I know that in the past I asked You into my life. I want to be Your child, I think and hope that I am your child, but I want to *know* that I am Your child. Lord, give me the reassurance that I have eternal life through You because of Your death on the cross for my sin (1 John 5:13).

- Now, which was the prayer of your heart? And why?

Spiritual Life

Check out these scriptures in your Bible. How do they *challenge* you as you face your day…and your life…and faithfully live out God's purpose for you?

Romans 8:29—

Romans 12:2—

2 Corinthians 4:16—

As you look at Hebrews 5:12, could these words have been written to and of you about your spiritual life? Please explain why or why not.

Continuing on with the challenge to nurture your spiritual life, how do these scriptures motivate you to pursue spiritual growth?

Matthew 4:4—

1 Corinthians 14:20—

Ephesians 4:14—

Ephesians 5:17—

2 Timothy 3:16-17—

Hebrews 5:12-14—

1 Peter 2:2—

2 Peter 3:18—

(I can't resist asking...what consistent resource did you observe regarding *how* spiritual growth occurs?)

Consider again the challenges of life...and particularly your life. What are three steps you can take on a regular basis to ensure your spiritual growth?

1.

2.

3.

Regarding strength to do what you purpose to do, what do these truths have to say?

Nehemiah 8:10—

Psalm 27:1 and 29:11—

Isaiah 40:31—

Philippians 4:13—

Think again about your God-ordained purposes in life and what it takes to faithfully live them out. How does a vibrant spiritual life help?

Practical Life

In a few sentences, describe your practical life in terms of…

Family life—(For instance, who are the people at home that make up your day, and what challenges do they present?)

Others—(Besides family, whose lives do you touch most often? In the neighborhood, at work, at school? Are you available to them? Are you actively involved in ministry to them?)

Physical life and health—(What physical demands are placed on you each day? And how's your health? Are you up for the challenge?)

Ministry life—(Again, besides family, who are those you serve, help, give to, or talk to about Jesus?)

Daily Life

Think about it…do you tend to live for the future, for tomorrow, putting things off, taking it easy, waiting until…(whatever!)? Or are you a "today" woman, giving your all today and refusing to eat "the bread of idleness" (Proverbs 31:27)? Are you striving to accomplish as much as you can for God, family, and others in your 1,440 minutes each day? See now for yourself these scriptures. How do they educate you, convict you, and motivate you regarding your daily life?

Luke 12:16-21—

James 4:13-15—

Read these verses in your Bible and then list at least one way to turn up the heat of your heart so that yours is…

    …a godly walk—Micah 6:8

    …a passionate walk—Philippians 3:13-14

    …a sober walk—Ephesians 5:15-16

    …a wise walk—Ephesians 5:17

Just for Today

Jonathan Edwards made five resolutions in his youth.
Number One on his list was
"Live with all my might while I do live."
Number Two on his list was
"Never lose one moment of time,
but improve it in the most profitable way possible."
(He died at 55.)

❧ *Just for today…*

❧ *Just for tomorrow…*

❧ *Just for this week…*

— Seeking a Heart of Wisdom —

Please read the "Seeking a Heart of Wisdom" section in your book again. As you consider the contents of this chapter and God's wisdom for your life as a woman, what one timeless principle or truth spoke to your heart…and what do you plan to do about it?

I Need Help with...
My Bible

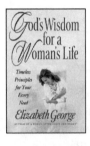

In your personal copy of *God's Wisdom for a Woman's Life* read the chapter titled "I Need Help with…My Bible." Make notes here about what from this chapter meant the most to you or offered you the greatest challenge or helped you grow in wisdom.

Before you begin this all-important lesson about God's Word, the Bible, look again at "The Three Stages of Bible Reading." Write out which stage best describes you and tell why.

The Treasure of God's Word

This study is about God's wisdom for your life. And where is that wisdom to be found? In the treasure of God's Word, the Bible! As one Bible teacher explains, "Before you try to obtain an object it is best to determine its source or where it can be found. If you desire food, you go to the grocery store where it is sold. If you want clothing, you go to the retailer who handles this type of merchandise. When it comes to wisdom, the Bible makes it very clear where the source is to be found. It is in God."[3]

Copy Proverbs 2:6 here from your Bible. Then read the explanatory words from several respected Bible commentators shared below.

> God is the fountain of all knowledge... "Wisdom," "knowledge," and "understanding"...comes, as it were, from his mouth to our ears (v. 2).[4]

> The wisdom of the Word brings us into a kind of life we never knew before. We find that the Lord is in the habit of providing wisdom, for He is its source (2:6). From God's mouth comes His Word, which gives us an intimate knowledge of Him as well as understanding, or discrimination in judgment.[5]

As you assess the importance and the power of the treasure of God's Word, consider these two scenarios.

> How did Jesus reprimand the religious group called the Sadducees in Matthew 22:29?

How is it that Daniel was able to interpret Nebuchadnezzar's dream according to Daniel 2:19-23?

Now look at Proverbs 2, verse 4. How strenuously do these scriptures say you are to look for the treasure of God's Word? In your own words, describe how tough this might be.

Recount now your last venture into the mine of God's Word in terms of time, energy, and passion. Did your efforts measure up to the challenge in Proverbs 2:4? Please explain your answer.

The Bible comes from God—You've looked at 2 Timothy 3:16 before, but read it again. What does this verse teach about the Bible?

And 2 Peter 1:21?

Now ponder this information.

> God is wisdom. God has wisdom. God is ready and willing to give you that wisdom if you will meet the conditions He has laid out in His Word. Out of His mouth, through the writings of holy men of God moved by the Holy Spirit, He has given us His

Word. That is the revelation of His knowledge and understanding. Beyond the shadow of a doubt, the greatest gift ever bestowed on the human race— apart from the salvation wrought by Jesus Christ, the living Word—is the Holy Bible, the written Word.[6]

Do you agree? And if so, how important does that make the habit of seeking out the treasure of God's Word?

The Bible causes you to grow in Christlikeness—Now read 2 Corinthians 3:18. What is its message to your heart?

Also, what do these scriptures teach you about *how* applying God's Word causes you to grow in Christlikeness?

Romans 12:2—

Ephesians 4:22-24—

2 Timothy 3:14-15—

The apostle Paul desired that his beloved friends in Ephesus would "grow up" in Christ. Read his exhortation for yourself in Ephesians 4:14-15. I regularly pray for myself that I might "grow up" in Christ. And, dear one, I pray the same for you, too. Now, the most important question is…do *you* pray this for yourself? Please make Paul's desire yours as well!

Unearthing the Treasure of God's Wisdom

Now that we know (and acknowledge) that God's Word is indeed treasure, how can we go about the business of unearthing that treasure?

Step 1: Read it—What example or wise advice do these people of the Bible have to pass on regarding the importance of reading God's Word, the Bible?

Moses in Exodus 24:7—

The king in Deuteronomy 17:19-20—

Joshua in Joshua 8:34-35—

Ezra in Nehemiah 8:1-3—

Isaiah in Isaiah 34:16—

Step 2: Study it—What example or wise advice do these people of the Bible have to pass on regarding the importance of studying God's Word, the Bible?

  Jesus in John 5:39—

  The Bereans in Acts 17:11—

Step 3: Hear it—From what wise and gifted people can you hear the Word of God…and where?

  Ephesians 4:11-12—

  Titus 2:3—

  Hebrews 10:24-25—

Step 4: Memorize it—How can God's Word hidden in your heart benefit your life?

  Joshua 1:8—

  Psalm 1:2-3—

  Psalm 37:31—

  Psalm 119:11—

Proverbs 2:1-2—

Step 5: Devour it—To delight means to take pleasure in and to enjoy! How did these saints devour God's Word, and what were its wondrous effects?

Job 23:12—

Jeremiah 15:16—

In your own words, summarize the significance of reading, studying, hearing, memorizing, and devouring the Bible. Then note your plan for making the treasure of God's wisdom yours.

Just for Today

Open the book of God
And read a portion there;
That it may hallow all thy thoughts,
And sweeten all thy care.[7]

❧ *Just for today...*

❦ *Just for tomorrow…*

❦ *Just for this week…*

Seeking a Heart of Wisdom

Please read the "Seeking a Heart of Wisdom" section in your book again. As you consider the contents of this chapter and God's wisdom for your life as a woman, what one timeless principle or truth spoke to your heart…and what do you plan to do about it?

I Need Help with... My Prayer Life

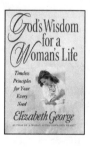

In your personal copy of *God's Wisdom for a Woman's Life* read the chapter titled "I Need Help with...My Prayer Life." Make notes here about what from this chapter meant the most to you or offered you the greatest challenge or helped you to grow in wisdom.

Before you head into the why's and how's of developing a prayer life, let's take your heart's temperature. It always helps to know what you are dealing with before you embark on bettering your life! Describe the last time you spent time *alone* in prayer (not with your husband, friend, Bible-study members, Sunday-school class, or Christian workmates or mothers' group). When (as in the date) was it, and what time of day was it? And where were you? About how long was your prayer time? Did you use any tools—

your Bible, a prayer journal, prayer guide, or hymn book? Make your notes below.

Developing a Prayer Life

Discipline is training that develops self-control, character, order-liness, or efficiency. I'm sure that's what you want when it comes to your prayer life! And as with any discipline, a dynamic prayer life must be carefully cultivated and developed. Look now at the kinds of efforts you can make in this vital area of prayer.

Do it!—How did David say to go about "doing it" when it came to the *when* of prayer in Psalm 5:3?

And in Psalm 55:17?

How did Jesus say to go about "doing it" when it came to the *where* of prayer in Matthew 6:6?

Do it badly—What did Jesus say about the "wrong" way to pray in Matthew 6:5 and 7?

Rather than being interested in a pat "formula" and eloquence in prayer, what was Jesus looking for instead according to Luke 18:9-14?

What truths can you make your own regarding "doing it" and "doing it badly" after reading these passages on prayer? List three.

    1.

    2.

    3.

Do it regularly—Let's go back to Psalm 55:17 and compare it with 1 Thessalonians 5:17. What is the message?

Hebrews 4:15-16—What is the message here?

Psalm 92:1-2—Regarding these words, someone has written, "Prayer is the key of the morning and the bolt of the night." How do these verses encourage regular prayer?

Do it faithfully—The statement was made in your book that prayer helps you to keep a clean slate with God. How do these scriptures encourage your faithfulness in confessing your sins in prayer?

    Psalm 66:18—

1 John 1:9—

Psalm 32:5—

Do it for life—In all things Jesus is always the perfect model. To the very end, what was His habit according to Luke 23:46 and 1 Peter 2:23?

Following a Model Prayer

What was the disciples' earnest plea to their Lord in Luke 11:1?

And, how did Jesus answer them in Luke 11:2-4?

Prayer is personal—What phrase from the Lord's Prayer teaches you this aspect about prayer?

According to these verses, what is the tender relationship Christians enjoy with God?

Matthew 6:4,6, and 8—

Matthew 7:11—

Galatians 4:6—

Prayer acknowledges God's reigning position—What phrase from the Lord's Prayer teaches you this aspect about prayer?

What further information regarding God's rule do you learn from Revelation 19:16?

Prayer acknowledges your trust—What phrase from the Lord's Prayer teaches you this aspect about prayer?

How did Jesus demonstrate His trust in Matthew 26:42?

Prayer indicates your dependence—What phrase from the Lord's Prayer teaches you this aspect about prayer?

How do these verses increase your awareness of your dependence upon God?

Psalm 23:1—

Psalm 37:25—

Matthew 6:25—

1 Timothy 6:8—

Prayer entreats God's guidance—What phrase from the Lord's Prayer teaches you this aspect about prayer?

How do these verses increase your understanding of God's guidance?

Psalm 23:2-3—

Psalm 32:8—

Psalm 121:8—

Proverbs 15:19—

James 1:5—

Following the Path of Discipline

Remember now the definition of the word *discipline* given earlier in this lesson. *Discipline* is training that develops self-control, character, orderliness, or efficiency. How do we go about developing the spiritual discipline of prayer? I made these statements regarding nurturing a discipline in my book *Life Management for Busy Women*. Read them now, and then I'll have a question for you to answer. I've used my author's prerogative and changed a few words to make it read more smoothly.

> Like in every woman's life, there are days when praying is your heart's delight. And there are days, too, when you do it because it is the right thing to do…and you know it…and it requires determination and a decision to do it. Beloved, that's the way it is with a discipline—any discipline. You do it because it is what you need to do and are supposed to do and because it is the right thing to do. You do it because it contributes to and propels you toward what you want to be and do…and in our case, that is becoming a woman marked by wisdom. And then…somehow…the duty of the discipline turns into sheer delight, and you reap the blessings of a priceless, tender relationship with the Lord a thousandfold.[8]

Now, my friend, note where you are in your quest for the hard-won discipline of regular prayer. And while you're at it, write out a "Prayer of Commitment" regarding following the path of greater discipline in your prayer life.

Just for Today

> The more you pray, the easier it becomes.
> The easier it becomes, the more you will pray.

❧ *Just for today...*

❧ *Just for tomorrow...*

❧ *Just for this week…*

Seeking a Heart of Wisdom

Please read the "Seeking a Heart of Wisdom" section in your book again. As you consider the contents of this chapter and God's wisdom for your life as a woman, what one timeless principle or truth spoke to your heart…and what do you plan to do about it?

6

I Need Help with...

My Spiritual Growth

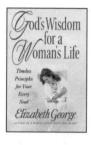

In your personal copy of *God's Wisdom for a Woman's Life* read the chapter titled "I Need Help with...My Spiritual Growth." Make notes here about what from this chapter meant the most to you or offered you the greatest challenge or helped you grow in wisdom.

Pursuing Spiritual Growth

Let's walk through this chapter now by first writing out each step for pursuing spiritual growth after its letter in the word **W-I-S-D-O-M.** Then answer the questions concerning each step.

W—

As was stated in your book, God's will is that you grow spiritually. How do these verses bear out this statement?

Ephesians 4:14-15—

2 Thessalonians 1:3—

1 Peter 2:2—

2 Peter 3:18—

Now look up these scriptures and note where spiritual life and spiritual growth begin.

Proverbs 9:10—

John 11:25—

Just in case you are unfamiliar with these truths, take a walk down what is called "The Romans Road." Note what each verse teaches about your spiritual life.

Romans 3:23—

Romans 6:23—

Romans 5:8—

Romans 10:9-10—

After this little "walk" do you consider yourself to be walking with Jesus Christ? (Please explain your answer.) If not, please look again at the prayers on page 27. Which one suits the need of your heart?

I—

It's good to know what God's Word, the Bible, has to say about sin. What do you learn in these verses?

Romans 3:23—

Romans 5:12—

1 John 1:8—

Once again, look at 1 Peter 2:1-2. How must sin be handled so that spiritual growth may occur?

(For your information, to "lay aside" means to put off as one puts off and lays aside a garment. Like you would strip off a soiled garment, so you must rid yourself of evil. As one scholarly source explains it, "There is a negative and purging phase in holiness."[9])

Revisit 1 John 1:9. What is its message regarding sin?

The wisdom of Proverbs offers you another help toward gaining wisdom in this area of sin. What does Proverbs 28:13 say it is?

S—
One of my favorite passages of Scripture details the plan of spiritual growth. I call it the "add to" passage. See it now for yourself in 2 Peter 1:5-8. What is this divine plan for growth? Answer by listing these seven add-ons of faith.

✓   ✓

✓   ✓

✓   ✓

✓

According to verse 8, what is the result of such diligent attention to spiritual growth?

We grow by the Word of God. What kind of appetite for God and His Word did these writers experience and express?

   Psalm 42:1-2—

   Psalm 63:1—

   Psalm 84:2—

Matthew 5:6—

How can such cravings be fulfilled, according to John 7:37?

Now, describe your appetite for God's Word in a few sentences. How does your desire to grow measure up to that of the writers of the scriptures just mentioned?

D—

As the age-old saying reminds us about all growth, you are either moving forward or backward; there is no such thing as standing still. What do these scriptures teach us about the ways and means of spiritual growth? (Hint: Note the verbs, the active part of each sentence.)

1 Corinthians 9:24—

Philippians 3:13-14—

2 Timothy 4:7—

Hebrews 12:1—

This step is called "**D**-ecide the method and rate of growth." So it's time to decide! Look again at the possibilities listed in your book. Then decide what you will do and set your personal goals to match up with the desires of your heart. For instance, I know some women who set a goal to do one thing each month to grow, such as listen through a series of teaching tapes, attend a Bible seminar or workshop, join a Bible study, enroll in a Bible class, read a helpful or "meaty" book. So…what's it going to be for you?

O—

We all need help with spiritual growth…and God is faithful to provide it!

> *Who* in the body of Christ is to help and teach the younger women in the church, according to Titus 2:3?

And *what kind* of woman is she to be (also verse 3)?

- •

- •

- •

And *what* is she to teach in a discipling relationship?

Verse 4: —

—

Verse 5: —

—

—

—

Now, *who* do you consider to be your "older women"?

And while we're at it, *who* do you consider to be your "younger women"?

Are any changes called for? Please explain.

M—
On a reading through the book of Psalms, I kept a record in my personal journal of every utterance of the two words "I will" that tumbled out of the heart and rolled off the pen of the individual psalmists. When I was done, believe me, I was well acquainted with the need for and the power of decisiveness! Note the spiritual discipline spoken of in just these few "I will's," and don't be surprised if they are familiar!

Psalm 5:3—   Psalm 119:8—

Psalm 55:17—   Psalm 119:16—

Psalm 63:1—

What decisions "will" you make to maintain your spiritual growth? Note them here. (And P.S.—Begin each one with the words "I will"!)

Just for Today

❧ *Just for today…*

❧ *Just for tomorrow…*

❧ *Just for this week…*

—*Seeking a Heart of Wisdom*—

Please read the "Seeking a Heart of Wisdom" section in your book again. As you consider the contents of this chapter and God's wisdom for your life as a woman, what one timeless principle or truth spoke to your heart…and what do you plan to do about it?

I Need Help with...
My Time

In your personal copy of *God's Wisdom for a Woman's Life* read the chapter titled "I Need Help...with My Time." Make notes here about what from this chapter meant the most to you or offered you the greatest challenge or helped you grow in wisdom.

Managing Your Life

Managing your life begins with knowing your priorities and learning how to prioritize them. The dictionary defines these terms as...

> ...*precedence in time, order, and importance,*

> ...*to arrange items in order of priority, and*

> ...*to assign an item to a particular level of priority*

Begin the better management of your life by making a list of God's priorities for a wise woman according to Titus 2:3-5. And if this passage is beginning to look familiar, *bravo!* It's a key text for God's plan for your life as a Christian woman.

When I think of making improvements, I always think of the maxim—a problem defined is a problem half solved! So...at first glance, as you look at your own life laid beside God's priority list, do you see any areas where your attention is lacking? If so, name them.

Prioritizing Your Time

Your book dealt with these priority uses of time. Consider each one of them now. And as you do, remember the definition of *priority* and *prioritize* (see previous page).

Time with God—How does Matthew 6:33 encourage you to make God and time with God your first priority...and what does it say about the other areas, issues, concerns, and duties of your life? Answer and then revisit this quotation regarding time at the beginning of this chapter in your book: "Take time for God—it is life's only lasting investment."

Time with your husband—If you are married, think back over this past week. How many minutes (you notice I didn't say hours!) have you and your husband been alone together? And if the minutes were few, why? What were the culprits?

What one thing can you do to improve in this important priority area and give it more time this week?

Time with your children—If you have children, again I ask you to evaluate the time you spent with each child this past week.

As a young mother I was supremely convicted when I learned that Susanna Wesley, the mother of John *and* Charles Wesley (and seventeen other children!—although several of them died before the age of two), spent one hour per week alone with each child. Now, what simple steps can you take to increase your time with each child? And while you're doing this exercise, keep in mind that the best thing a mother can spend on her children is time—not money!

Time with family and friends—I once read this penetrating thought (or was it meant to be a joke?): "Isn't it aggravating how little value other people put on your time?" Once again, evaluate the amount of time you are spending with family and friends. How does this time compare with the time you are spending with your husband and children? Are your husband and children receiving the bulk of your time in comparison to others? Is some reassignment of time needed?

Time with your self—With your busy schedule, time is limited. Where in your day could you find 15 minutes to be alone to recharge your batteries? And what would you do in that 15 minutes? (Again, don't forget to look at the quotation at the front of this chapter in your book! I just read through it again and saw such wonderful recharging activities as "Take time to think—it is the source of power. Take time to read— it is the fountain of wisdom.")

Time for the unexpected—I'm chuckling as I'm reading that Henry Kissinger, while he served as secretary of state, said, "There can't be a crisis next week. There's no time in my schedule!"[10] It's funny, isn't it, how we think we are in control of our schedules? But reality teaches us differently. Plan as we may, our plans may be (and probably will be!) interrupted, changed, altered, and many times thrown out altogether. How are you when it comes to handling the unexpected? And what is your attitude when changes emerge?

Behold now the Master, how Jesus handled an "interruption" to His plan to withdraw and pray after learning of John the Baptist's death. First, what was the interruption and how did Jesus respond in Matthew 14:13-14? Then note how this episode ended in verses 22 and 23.

Make note of several lessons you can learn from the Master about graciously managing interruptions. Then take them with you into your next day.

Time for planning—It's been said, "Either you plan your day, or someone else will be glad to plan it for you." And, "God has a wonderful plan for your life, and so does everyone else!" It's also been recommended that you spend at least five minutes each morning planning your day before you begin it. I personally plan at least 15 minutes each morning and 30 minutes several times during each week. Now, I ask you, where in your day can you set aside a few minutes to plan? (Hint—a good time to think about this is the night before!)

Do you need to purchase a yearly planner or a planner pad that allows you to tear off each day, week, or month? Or can you print one off the Internet? What other tools could help you become a better and wiser planner?

Time for work—What standard items do you need to carry with you each day to your workplace or school or on your errands? Take time to think through your days and make an all-inclusive list. Then consider how your revealing answers to this one question can free your time up each morning as you prepare for your work. And, how much preparation can you do the night before?

Beloved, as every thread of gold is valuable, so is every moment of your time! And that's why prioritizing your time is essential to gaining wisdom. The psalmist prayed to gain a heart of wisdom. How was he planning to move toward such a cherished prize? By numbering his days (Psalm 90:12). The apostle Paul prayed to redeem time. And how was he planning to do that? By walking carefully and wisely, by watching over his minutes (Colossians 4:5). Now, what is the prayer of your heart regarding planning, prioritizing, and practicing your priorities so that you have time with God, with loved ones, for yourself, for others, and for your work?

Learning What's Important

Briefly, as we end this lesson, how can you:

Learn to be more effective—Based on the priorities addressed in this lesson, do you consider yourself to be efficient or effective...or neither? Please explain.

Learn to eliminate—What is your answer to the question, *What can be eliminated from my life at this time that is not a priority?* Be honest...and be ruthless!

Just for Today

❧ *Just for today...*

❧ *Just for tomorrow...*

❧ *Just for this week...*

Seeking a Heart of Wisdom

Please read the "Seeking a Heart of Wisdom" section in your book again. As you consider the contents of this chapter and God's wisdom for your life as a woman, what one timeless principle or truth spoke to your heart...and what do you plan to do about it?

I Need Help with...
$\mathcal{M}$y $\mathcal{S}$chedule

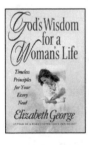

In your personal copy of *God's Wisdom for a Woman's Life* read the chapter titled "I Need Help with…My Schedule." Make notes here about what from this chapter meant the most to you or offered you the greatest challenge or helped you grow in wisdom.

In chapter 8 in your book I shared about how my friend Julie changed my life with a few wise words. Well, I've been doubly blessed! God also gave me another life-changing friend who at one time studied under the famous Peter Drucker, prominent management authority and the "father of effective management." Believe me, she had a lot to teach me about time and life management! About planning, scheduling, and executing mountains of work! Her mentor, Dr. Drucker, said this: "Nothing so much distinguishes effective executives as their tender loving care of time….Those executives who really get things done don't start with their work: they start with their time."[11]

Are you wondering how this information about "effective executives" relates to you? Well, I'm glad you asked! When I think of you (and me), I think of an executive, a CEO, head of operations, a manager. You are entrusted by God to manage not only your own life but the lives of those you live with. You are also to oversee your productivity, your body, your spiritual growth, your service to God, your schoolwork, your work…and the list of management responsibilities goes on! Plus you've been given the oversight of the most important institution in the world—a home!

Catch the vision, dear one! *You* are to be an "effective executive"! *You* are to be distinguished by your "tender loving care of time." *You* are to really get things done by starting with the scheduling of your time…so that the work gets done. So I'm asking *you* to roll up your "executive shirtsleeves," put on your thinking cap, hang a "Manager" sign on your door, and master the fine art of scheduling!

"A List of Projected Operations"

What is a schedule?—Copy out of your book the dictionary definition of *schedule* here.

What is your schedule?—Now think about your "projected operations" for this week. Based on what we are learning in our book about living a life of wisdom, what are they? What do you wish to accomplish…and what must you accomplish? Make a list here.

Solomon, the wisest person who ever lived before Christ, made a schedule. What is one "operation" he came up with on his "projected operations" list in 1 Kings 4:7? And what can you learn about scheduling from Solomon's wise solution?

Why have a schedule?—Note these three reasons.

1. *God's purpose*—See for yourself Acts 27:22-25. The apostle Paul considered himself to belong to God. And he considered serving God and worshiping God to be his purpose in life. How do the following scriptures help you relate to Paul's passionate perception of his life and God's purpose?

   Ephesians 1:11—

   Colossians 1:16—

   Romans 8:28—

   2 Timothy 1:9—

As you go about your daily business and the operations of your life, how much do you think about God's purpose for your life? For your day? For your work? What adjustments are called for?

2. *Your manner*—Several proverbs point to the poor results, emotions, and chaos that can permeate a day with no plan. In a few words, note each proverb's message.

Proverbs 13:4a—

Proverbs 15:19a—

Proverbs 19:2b—

Proverbs 19:15—

Proverbs 20:4—

Proverbs 20:13a—

Proverbs 21:5—

Proverbs 24:30-31—

Can you think of a day when you actually created a fairly good schedule? How was your emotional state during the day? At the end of that day? And was a decent amount of work accomplished?

3. *The matter of wisdom*—Look up the specific verses referred to in Proverbs 31. What do these teach you about the *priorities* of a wise woman?

Proverbs 31:30—

Proverbs 31:13-15—

Proverbs 31:27—

Proverbs 31:20—

What do these teach about her *schedule?*

Proverbs 31:15—

Proverbs 31:27—

Proverbs 31:18—

Every woman needs a guide, a model, a mentor, or an example. Here in Proverbs 31 God gives you one! What lessons will you take away from her life?

Creating an Arrangement

In the book *God's Wisdom for a Woman's Life,* I shared about learning how to create beautiful floral arrangements by positioning the flowers properly. In a similar way, we need to position certain parts of our schedule properly. Read Ecclesiastes 3:1-9. King Solomon speaks of the predictable "operations" in life. He observes that our lives run on a schedule, by routine, or in a cycle. They have a set scheme and appointed times. Now read my list of daily "times."

The Daily Times

There is a time to get up…
and a time to go to bed.
There is a time to work…
and a time to rest.
There is a time to seek God…
and a time to serve God.
There is a time to set up…
and a time to act.
There is a time to prepare…
and a time to execute.
There is a time to plan…
and a time to carry out those plans.
There is a time to pray…
and a time to move out.
There is a time to produce…
and a time to play.
There is a time to care for others…
and a time to be cared for by others.
There is a time to live for Christ…
and a time to die as gain.

What does your set scheme of things, your schedule, look like? Are you creating an arrangement by organizing the events of your life in some sort of schedule, or are you merely allowing life to happen to you? Share your observations of your "Daily Times" here.

Creating a Schedule

Now it's time to create your schedule for just one day. Follow these steps and check when done.

Step 1—Write down a time when you will meet with *God*. Place that first on your fresh, blank schedule. _____

Step 2—Who are the *people* in your life? What will you do for them, and when? Transfer this information to your schedule. _____

Step 3—Make a list of your *future* events. Place them on your calendar. Then write down what you can do today in preparation for these future events. Write these activities on your schedule. _____

Step 4—What will or must you do for your *self?* As usual, make notes and schedule in yourself, even if only a five-minute slot is open. _____

Step 5—You'll surely be graduating to weekly, monthly, and yearly scheduling soon! Then, dear one, you'll witness your "projected operations," lovingly and carefully tended to day by day, blossom into a bold and beautiful future that is marked by wisdom and honors your Lord!

Just for Today

❧ *Just for today...*

❧ *Just for tomorrow...*

❧ *Just for this week...*

Seeking a Heart of Wisdom

Please read the "Seeking a Heart of Wisdom" section in your book again. As you consider the contents of this chapter and God's wisdom for your life as a woman, what one timeless principle or truth spoke to your heart...and what do you plan to do about it?

9

I Need Help with...
My *H*ome

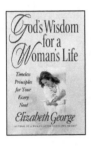

In your personal copy of *God's Wisdom for a Woman's Life* read the chapter titled "I Need Help with...My Home." Make notes here about what from this chapter meant the most to you or offered you the greatest challenge or helped you grow in wisdom.

As I began writing our chapter on home, I couldn't help but pay a small tribute to my dear mother. Indeed, I never say or hear or read the word *home* without thinking of her. And now I want you to take a minute and think of your mother. What are some lessons on home that she instilled in you? Think about your meals, your holidays, her dishes, even her pots and pans. Picture her in her kitchen (...even if it was only to make a cup of tea!). Remember her favorite recipes, the "dishes" she's famous for. And remember her hobbies, too—what she loved to do. I know not every woman has 100 percent fond memories of her mother. But I also believe that there is something—something!—that you can put your finger on that your mom imparted to you and blessed you with in the Home Department. And after you've done the remembering (and perhaps a little sniffling, too), if she's still living, write her a card and express your appreciation. No, not an email. A card or a letter! I guarantee you, she'll save it!

A Home Must Be Built

> A house is built of logs and stones,
> Of tiles and posts and tiers;
> A home is built of loving deeds
> That stand a thousand years.[12]

As we begin to focus on "building" a home and "home building," look up these key verses in your favorite Bible and make note of God's message through them to your heart.

Proverbs 9:1—

Proverbs 14:1—

Proverbs 24:3-4—

Proverbs 31:27—

Prayer—Every woman needs help with her home-making. And there's no doubt that prayer is Help with a capital H! How do these verses encourage you to pray about your home, a most "daily" item on your must-do list?

Ephesians 5:20—

Philippians 4:6-7—

1 Thessalonians 5:17—

1 Thessalonians 5:18—

I often teach that prayer lifts home-making out of the physical sphere and transports it into the spiritual. Do you agree or disagree? And have you tried it? If not, try it...and then share what difference praying about your home, your home-making, and the people in your home made in your attitude and efforts.

Resolution—How do these powerful and instructive scriptures help you in the Resolution Department?

Ecclesiastes 9:10—

Romans 12:11—

Philippians 3:13-14—

Colossians 3:17—

Colossians 3:23—

Here's how I got started down this path of resolve—I wrote out the following "I Wills."

The Heart of a Homemaker

1. I will get up before my family, in order to prepare myself spiritually and physically.

2. I will prepare breakfast for my family and sit with them while they eat.

3. I will work diligently to send every member of my family off in a good mood.

4. I will consult my husband every day to see if there is anything special he wants me to do for him.

5. I will keep a neat and orderly home.

6. I will respond positively.

7. I will personally meet and greet each family member as he or she returns home.

8. I will prepare special, good food for my family.

9. I will make dinner a special time.

10. I will grow daily in the areas of the Lord, marriage, family, and homemaking.[13]

Now it's your turn to write your own set of ten homemaking "I Wills." Write them down…and don't forget to begin each one with the words "I Will."

1.

2.

3.

4.

5.

6.

7.

8.

9.

10.

Presence—One of my maxims for life is "Nothing grand just happens." And is this ever true when it comes to the home! Friend, we simply must be there, be present, and be *all* there when we are there. I know time is limited. And I know that we have a multitude of responsibilities and roles, and we wear a variety of hats. But I ask you now, list three things you can give up in order to be present at home more often.

—

—

—

Next list three things you can give up while you *are* at home (television? telephone? hobbies?) that are robbing you of time and energy for your home-making.

—

—

—

Time—Now, how do you think one extra hour at home each day—or one extra hour of *work* while you are at home each day (if that's your case!)—will generate or create many wonderful "home improvements"?

Notice now how *time* was spent—and mis-spent!—in these passages from Proverbs, the Book of Wisdom.

Proverbs 6:6-11—

Proverbs 24:30-34—

A Home Is Built with Care

It's time for a few opposites. We've been considering the positive elements that go into building a home. Now take a look at some home-wreckers. As usual, read each scripture in your Bible. Then note the behavior that is a detriment to a woman's desire to fulfill God's assignment to build a home.

Proverbs 14:1—

How do you think this is done, and how do you think it is a detriment?

Proverbs 31:27—

How do you think this is a detriment?

Just for Today

🥀 *Just for today...*

🥀 *Just for tomorrow...*

🥀 *Just for this week...*

Seeking a Heart of Wisdom

Please read the "Seeking a Heart of Wisdom" section in your book again. As you consider the contents of this chapter and God's wisdom for your life as a woman, what one timeless principle or truth spoke to your heart…and what do you plan to do about it?

I Need Help with...
My *M*arriage

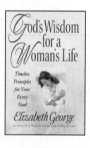

In your personal copy of *God's Wisdom for a Woman's Life* read the chapter titled "I Need Help with...My Marriage." Make notes here about what from this chapter meant the most to you or offered you the greatest challenge or helped you grow in wisdom.

Ten Timeless Principles for a Wife

1. *Work as a team*—What does Genesis 2:18 say about God's idea of teamwork?

In the following scriptures, how does the wife contribute to the teamwork of her marriage?

Proverbs 31:12 and 31—

Acts 18:3—

Name one key way you could become a better "team player" with your husband. (And P.S.—It never hurts to ask your husband!)

2. *Learn to communicate*—Write out these verses on communication. Which ones should you commit to memory and how will you apply them to yourself?

Proverbs 10:19—

Proverbs 15:1—

Proverbs 16:21—

James 1:19—

3. *Enjoy intimacy*—In your Bible, look up these why's and how's of sexual intimacy. How does each truth help your understanding of the importance and beauty of the physical aspect of a marriage relationship?

   Proclaimed—Genesis 2:24-25

   Procreation—Genesis 1:27-28

   Pleasure—Proverbs 5:15-19

   Purity—1 Corinthians 7:2

   Hebrews 13:4

   Partnership—1 Corinthians 7:3-4

   Protection—1 Corinthians 7:5

   Intimacy in marriage is a wonderful gift from God. But, like all good things, it doesn't just happen. Intimacy takes time and effort. What one thing can you do to create new opportunities?

4. *Manage money*—Due to your position and role in the family, you are often, if not daily, put in the position of managing all or part of the family finances. You are a *steward*—one placed in a position of responsibility. The Bible says in 1 Corinthians 4:2 that a steward is to be found faithful or trustworthy. How would you describe your money management and stewardship to this point? What one thing can

you do to improve in this vital area of your marriage? What do you and your husband need to discuss regarding finances?

5. *Keep up the home*—You, dear wife, provide a ministry (and more!) to those who dwell within your home-sweet-home when you keep up the home. How would you rate yourself as a home-lover and home-keeper (Titus 2:5)? And how do you think your husband would rate you? What one major change must be made?

6. *Raise your children*—By working together as a team in raising your children, you and your husband provide consistency in discipline and structure for the family. One of the most devastating examples of poor parenting is found in the biblical couple Isaac and Rebekah. What colossal error did they make in raising Jacob and Esau in Genesis 25:28?

Effective childraising involves both parents. What are a few simple instructions found in Ephesians 6:4? (And note: The word "fathers" also has the meaning of "parents.")

And in Proverbs 22:6?

7. *Make time for fun*—Describe the last time you and your husband had fun together. Now plan for the next time! (It took a little doing for my Jim and me, but we now have two kayaks for spontaneous fun and paddling adventures on the water near our home. What will it take for you?)

Just for "fun," what activities did the happy couple in Song of Solomon 7:11-12 enjoy?

8. *Serve the Lord*—We've already looked at Priscilla and Aquila as they worked together as a team (see Principle #1). Now describe this couple's service to the Lord and His people as shown in Romans 16:3-5.

What can you and your husband do together to serve the Lord? Can you open your home for a Bible study? Can you serve at the next social? Can you host a missionary overnight? Can you give more of your money? List some possibilities here and pray for a time to share them with your husband.

9. *Reach out to others*—Once again we must turn our attention to our dynamic duo, Priscilla and Aquila. Wow, what a contribution they made in their day as they worked as a team in their business and as they ministered together! Now see Acts 18:24-26 and witness them reaching out to another. Who, why, and how did they reach out...and what was the dynamic result (verses 27-28)?

What is said about hospitality in...

...Romans 12:9,13?

...Titus 1:7-8?

...1 Peter 4:9?

What are some times and events when you and your husband can plan to open your home and reach out to those in your neighborhood?

In your church?

From your workplace?

(And P.S.—Be sure you make this a team project!)

10. *Grow in the Lord*—In your book this timeless principle appears in the "Seeking a Heart of Wisdom" section. How do you think your faithful nurturing of your spiritual growth makes a difference in your relationship with your husband?

As you think about your growth in the Lord, how can you (in the words of TV Chef Emeril) "kick it up a notch"? List three growth exercises you will put into place.

—

—

—

Just for Today

❧ *Just for today…*

❧ *Just for tomorrow…*

❧ *Just for this week…*

Seeking a Heart of Wisdom

Please read the "Seeking a Heart of Wisdom" section in your book again. As you consider the contents of this chapter and God's wisdom for your life as a woman, what one timeless principle or truth spoke to your heart...and what do you plan to do about it?

I Need Help with...
My Children

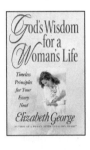

In your personal copy of *God's Wisdom for a Woman's Life* read the chapter titled "I Need Help with...My Children." Make notes here about what from this chapter meant the most to you or offered you the greatest challenge or helped you grow in wisdom.

Wisdom from a Godly Mother

Amazingly, God gives His mothers the help they need...if they desire it. I needed wisdom, I knew it, and I went looking for it. And I can only thank God that He has paraded woman after woman (or should I say mother after mother?) across my path over the years to feed me with God's wisdom and timeless principles for what I consider to be life's most challenging responsibility—raising children!

Now for you. I have two questions.

1. Are you a mom, one with a handful of children or a kit-and-caboodle of them? And their ages don't matter! If so, are you looking for help? I hope so, because the desire for instruction is a mark of wisdom. Make a list of those who assist you regularly with your childraising quandaries and questions. Be sure and thank God for those who co-labor with you in this vital area.

   If you are uncertain where to turn, what direction does the Bible give you in Titus 2:3-4?

   Now make a list of those you could ask for help. Pray...and then approach them. It's as simple as, "I've got a question I'd like to ask you," or "I've got a situation I'd like your advice on."

   What does the Bible say about seeking advice in...

   ...Proverbs 12:15?

   ...Proverbs 15:22?

   ...Proverbs 19:20?

…Proverbs 20:18?

(And P.S.—While you're gathering wisdom, don't forget to read. That's where I found some much-needed help! Make it a habit to ask others for titles of good and godly books about raising your children.)

2. Are you an older mom with a little experience under your belt or a seasoned mother who has raised her children? Then God has an assignment for you…and it's found in Titus 2:3-4 also. What is it God wants you to do?

How can you make yourself more available to other mothers?

And here's another assignment. Write down your child-raising principles. That way you will have them ready to pass on to others.

Wisdom from God

Are you yet in the habit of reading one chapter from the book of Proverbs every day? That is, the chapter that corresponds with the date of the month? As I'm writing, it is the nineteenth day of the month. That means it's the day I read Proverbs 19. This one habit will make a difference in not only each day, but in the direction your life takes as you walk on the path of daily wisdom. Stop now and read the "Proverbs for the day." Check here when done, and then note one thing you learned or some wisdom that was gained for your life. _____

Ten Timeless Principles for Childraising

1. *Teach your children*—Begin by reading these proverbs and noting their messages to mothers.

   Proverbs 1:8—

   Proverbs 6:20—

   Proverbs 31:1—

   Here's another basic scripture regarding teaching your children. As you read Deuteronomy 6:6-7, note this information:

   Who is to do the teaching?

   What is to be taught?

   Where is the teaching to take place?

   When is the teaching to take place?

And here's a bonus question: *What* is the prerequisite for the teacher (verse 5)?

2. *Train your children*—The Bible clearly instructs parents to train their children for the Lord and His purposes. What does Proverbs 22:6 have to say?

In your book we considered the requirements for training children. Now, how's...

...your heart of obedience?

...your heart of faith?

...your heart of dedication?

How can you turn up the heat in your heart if the fire is flickering and fading? List at least three steps.

—

—

—

In chapter 7 I mentioned Susanna Wesley as the mother of nineteen children, including Christianity's famous brothers John and Charles. Mother-par-excellence, Susanna had a list of rules for raising and training her children. Before you read her "Rules" on the next page, let me ask again, do you have any written rules for childraising? Do you have a set of guiding principles and practices? Are there certain scriptures (especially the wisdom from Proverbs!) upon which you base your childraising? If not, start your own list here and now. Jot down five principles to begin your list and revisit it later.

—

—

—

—

—

Susanna's Rules for Raising Children

1. Allow no eating between meals.

2. Put all children in bed by eight o'clock.

3. Require them to take medicine without complaining.

4. Subdue self-will in a child and thus work together with God to save his soul.

5. Teach each one to pray as soon as he can speak.

6. Require all to be still during family worship.

7. Give them nothing that they cry for, and only that which they ask for politely.

8. To prevent lying, punish no fault which is first confessed and repented of.

9. Never allow a sinful act to go unpunished.

10. Never punish a child twice for a single offense.

11. Commend and reward good behavior.

12. Any attempt to please, even if poorly performed, should be commended.

13. Preserve property rights, even in the smallest matters.

14. Strictly observe all promises.

15. Require no daughter to work before she can read well.

16. Teach children to fear the rod.[14]

(And by the way, Susanna Wesley's list has now been in print for over 200 years. Who knows? Perhaps your list will be the one to help generations of mothers for the next 200 years!)

3. *Instruct them*—Scan through these instances of parental instruction. Briefly, what was the instruction?

    Proverbs 1:10-19—

    Proverbs 7:1-27—

    Proverbs 31:1-9—

How seriously must you take God's instruction to you to instruct your children? Are any changes called for?

4. *Correct them*—To get you started down this path, what do these proverbs teach you about correcting your children?

    Proverbs 13:24—   Proverbs 23:13—

    Proverbs 19:18—   Proverbs 29:15—

    Proverbs 22:15—

Just for Today

❧ *Just for today…*

❧ *Just for tomorrow…*

❧ *Just for this week…*

Seeking a Heart of Wisdom

Please read the "Seeking a Heart of Wisdom" section in your book again. As you consider the contents of this chapter and God's wisdom for your life as a woman, what one timeless principle or truth spoke to your heart…and what do you plan to do about it?

12

I Need More Help with...
My Children

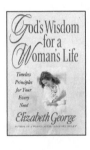

In your personal copy of *God's Wisdom for a Woman's Life* read the chapter titled "I Need More Help with...My Children." Make notes here about what from this chapter meant the most to you or offered you the greatest challenge or helped you grow in wisdom.

Before you begin this lesson, look back at the previous one and copy out the first four of the...

Ten Timeless Principles for Childraising

1.

2.

   3.

   4.

Now let's continue on with...

5. *Cherish your children*—The "older women" of Titus 2:3 were to admonish the younger women to "love their children" (verse 4). This word for love means to have affection for or to cherish one's children. Take a minute to think back through the past week, through yesterday, even through this very morning. What are you doing in your relationships with your children that would indicate to each one of them that he or she is cherished? Try to think of several efforts, kindnesses, or choices you made that conveyed your love, your fondness, and your appreciation for your beloved children. I know this is quite an assignment, but your time spent in remembering and pinpointing the actions of your heart will be well spent...and revealing! And even if your children are grown, go ahead and do the exercise. After all, "once a mother, always a mother." And if you have precious grandchildren, they, too, need to know of your love.

Hannah is an outstanding example of a loving mother. Yet her love played out in a most unusual way. Read her story now in 1 Samuel 1:9-11 and 20-28. What is your response to Hannah's willingness, if given a male child, to dedicate that child to the Lord?

I asked two questions in your book regarding your children, and I'm repeating them here. Do your best to answer them now. (And P.S.—It never hurts to talk to each child about such important things.) And take heart! If you come up short, make plans to pay greater attention to these areas, ask God for His help, and follow through.

—Does each of your children know he or she is cherished, well loved, and precious to you?

—In your heart, is each of your children "dedicated" to God?

6. *Take care of them*—Read about God's care for us in Matthew 6:25-32. This is a picture of the kind of care we should provide for our children. What steps did the Proverbs 31 woman take to care for the physical needs of her children in Proverbs 31:13-22?

Do your efforts in providing for your children's physical needs measure up? Are there any changes, corrections, or additions that must be made?

And just a note: Care for your children starts before they are born and continues through their years under your roof…and beyond. One of your greatest means of caring for all aspects of your children's lives is through your faithful prayers. You just may well be the only person on the face of this earth who is praying for them. So…be faithful to pray!

7. *Pay attention to them*—Life can be busy and complicated. In the hustle and bustle of daily life and living, children can get lost in the shuffle. But your children need to know that they come first. Take advantage of these priceless moments that are available, whether at mealtimes, bedtimes, playtimes, helping-with-homework-times, or attending school functions. Your children grow up all too quickly, and before you know it, these opportunities are gone. So while you have a chance, pay attention to your children. Do some or all of the following things this week. Check when they are done. Then journal or make a record of the response of the children. And even if there is no visible or verbal response, that's okay. Because maybe, just maybe(!), when they are older, they will pay attention to you.

_____Read a story.

_____Send an "I love you" note in their lunches.

_____Take them on a special outing.

_____Have an extra cuddle time while getting ready for bed.

_____Take each one on a special outing alone.

_____Hug your child three times a day and say "I love you!"

_____Have a heart-to-heart talk with an older child, a "How are you really doing?" talk.

8. *Demand peace in your home*—Read again about "The Three C's" and look them up in the book of Proverbs.

   C-asting lots—Proverbs 18:18. How might this practice help to keep the peace around your house?

   C-orrect—Proverbs 29:17. Proverbs also contains numerous verses on the subject of discipline and correction. What seems to be the consistent positive result of discipline according to…

   …Proverbs 3:11-12?

   …Proverbs 12:1?

   …Proverbs 13:1?

   …Proverbs 29:15?

   C-asting out—Proverbs 22:10. As one scholar explains, "Disagreement…sometimes arises not from the facts of a situation but from a *person* with a wrong attitude, who makes mischief."[15] How might this practice help to keep the peace around your house?

9. *Require respect from them*—Respect and honor of parents and authority is vital to raising godly children. What is the fifth of the Ten Commandments (Exodus 20:12)?

Look at Ephesians 6:1-3. Note how the apostle Paul personalized this command. What is its promise if obeyed?

What actions can hinder this training in respect (Ephesians 6:4)?

How high do you consider your children's respect level to be when it comes to you as a parent? And what first step can you take to up that level?

And speaking of respect, how do your children see you living out Ephesians 5:33?

10. *Be patient with them*—If you are a parent, you know that raising children is not easy, and it seems to be getting harder than ever to raise God-fearing children in a godless world. How are we to do this? There's no doubt that patience plays a big role. And where does patience come from according to Galatians 5:22-23?

And what does patience (and wisdom!) do according to…

   …Proverbs 15:2?

   …Proverbs 15:18?

   …Proverbs 15:28?

   …Proverbs 29:22?

Just for Today

❧ *Just for today…*

❧ *Just for tomorrow…*

❧ *Just for this week…*

Seeking a Heart of Wisdom

Please read the "Seeking a Heart of Wisdom" section in your book again. As you consider the contents of this chapter and God's wisdom for your life as a woman, what one timeless principle or truth spoke to your heart…and what do you plan to do about it?

13

I Need Help with...
My Appearance

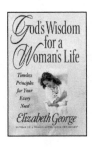

In your personal copy of *God's Wisdom for a Woman's Life* read the chapter titled "I Need Help with…My Appearance." Make notes here about what from this chapter meant the most to you or offered you the greatest challenge or helped you grow in wisdom.

Can you relate to the two women I heard discussing a television talk show on looks, beauty, appearance, and self-image? And now I ask you, how many times a day do you think about your appearance? Go a step further and note your nagging worries and concerns regarding your appearance.

ımeless Beauty Tips

#1. *True beauty is internal*—If you are a child of God through Jesus Christ, then Christ has secured for you what many refer to as your "position in Christ." What do these truths reveal about that position in Him?

2 Corinthians 5:17—

Ephesians 1:13—

Ephesians 2:4-5—

Colossians 1:13—

How can remembering who you are in Christ correct any unworthy and untrue thoughts you may have about yourself?

#2. *True beauty is enhanced by spiritual growth*—What harsh reality do you find in 2 Corinthians 4:16 regarding your physical body?

And what refreshing truth do you find there?

How does this take place (verse 18)?

I mentioned Proverbs 31:25 in this section of the chapter. Look at it now for yourself in your Bible. In fact, copy it here.

Can you name a handful of women you know who live out the truth of this scripture? Jot their names down. Thank God for them. Then pray for them. And as a final assignment, write them each a note of thanks and appreciation and encouragement. It takes courage and discipline to live a godly life. You can be sure your notes will give them a ray of hope!

Meet Rebekah—Here is beauty…and "beauty" in action! Read Rebekah's story in Genesis 24:12-25. How does the Bible describe Rebekah's physical beauty?

And how does the Bible detail the actions that revealed her "beauty" of graciousness, mercy, compassion, energy, voluntary service, and helpfulness?

How are you currently, or can you improve in, following in Rebekah's beautiful footsteps? (And here's a hint: You cannot be consumed with yourself and with others at the same time! It is one or the other! Other-oriented women are women who do not selfishly and self-centeredly think about themselves.)

Bonus question—What does the New Testament say about the beauty of "good works" in 1 Timothy 2:9-10?

#3. *True beauty is a matter of the heart*—In your Bible read 1 Peter 3:3-4. What strikes you most?

And what is your response to these phrases? (And please, write in the wording of these phrases from your favorite version of the Bible.)

...the hidden person of the heart (verse 4)

...the incorruptible ornament (verse 4)

...a gentle and quiet spirit (verse 4)

...very precious in the sight of God (verse 4)

When it comes to your outward appearance, how does
1 Samuel 16:7 help?

The Misuse of Beauty

We surely won't take long on this exercise(!), but look at the following blatant misuses of beauty. In each instance, make note of
the indicators of the heart of each woman and how she used
her beauty for evil.

Proverbs 5:3-8—

Proverbs 6:24-26—

Proverbs 7:5-21—

Proverbs 11:22—

What positive guidelines for your appearance can you draw
from the above negative examples?

Checklist for Your Heart

Check out your "clothing." Does it match up to God's instruction? For every "spiritual garment" (so to speak), list one way you can pay greater attention to it. (And don't forget to look at each verse in your Bible. You may also substitute the wording from your favorite Bible.)

✓ Put on…tender mercies (Colossians 3:12).

✓ Put on…kindness (Colossians 3:12).

✓ Put on…humbleness of mind (Colossians 3:12).

✓ Put on…meekness (Colossians 3:12).

✓ Put on…longsuffering (Colossians 3:12).

✓ Put on…a gentle and quiet spirit (1 Peter 3:4).

✓ Put on…a cloak of humility (1 Peter 5:5).

Now, what is the exhortation of Romans 13:14, and how would it help you with this "wardrobe" assignment?

Just for Today

A dear elderly Christian woman, distinguished for her youthful appearance, was asked what she used to preserve her charms. She replied sweetly,

I used for the lips, truth;
for the voice, prayer;
for the eyes, pity;
for the hand, charity;
for the figure, uprightness; and
for the heart, love.[16]

❧ *Just for today…*

❧ *Just for tomorrow…*

❧ *Just for this week…*

Seeking a Heart of Wisdom

Please read the "Seeking a Heart of Wisdom" section in your book again. As you consider the contents of this chapter and God's wisdom for your life as a woman, what one timeless principle or truth spoke to your heart…and what do you plan to do about it?

I Need More Help with...
My Appearance

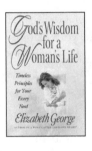

In your personal copy of *God's Wisdom for a Woman's Life* read the chapter titled "I Need More Help with...My Appearance." Make notes here about what from this chapter meant the most to you or offered you the greatest challenge or helped you grow in wisdom.

Timeless Beauty Tips

Before we begin this second lesson on God's wisdom regarding your appearance, revisit the previous lesson. Then write out its timeless principles for appearance.

#1—

#2—

#3—

More Timeless Beauty Tips

As a woman, I'm sure you've already been exposed to a lifetime of "beauty tips." Indeed, every grocery store checkout line bombards you with magazine covers heralding some new beauty treatment, invention, or diet! And if you have daughters…well, suffice it to say, you are entering Round #2 as they begin to delve into cosmetology. Truly…it is a girl thing!

But as one of God's wise women, and as one of God's wise mothers(!), you want to practice—and impart to your daughters—God's timeless principles and "beauty tips" for your appearance. Let's continue on discovering more about His wisdom regarding this most practical and daily issue in every woman's life.

#4. *True beauty is also external*—So far we've focused on the internals of true beauty, on the inner person of the heart, and on nurturing a beautiful heart. Now, for a few externals! As you begin this section of your study, look again in your Bible at 1 Timothy 2:9-10. Keep it handy as you move through this section.

   Modesty—What dress standard do these verses set regarding modesty?

   1 Timothy 2:9—

   Titus 2:5—

   1 Peter 3:3—

And how was a failure in the Modesty Department lived out in Proverbs 7:10?

Propriety—I know there's a repeat or two here, but look again at these verses and note their message about propriety.

1 Timothy 2:9—

Proverbs 31:25—

What is to be your motivation for propriety in your appearance according to Proverbs 31:30?

Humility was mentioned as an ingredient in propriety. What do these favorite scriptures remind you about humility?

Philippians 2:5,8—

1 Peter 5:6—

Colossians 3:12—

Moderation—As your first exercise, copy out 1 Timothy 2:9 from your Bible.

According to this verse, how were the women of Paul and Timothy's day obviously in violation of this principle of moderation?

We noted the element of self-control. Why would self-control be called for in the Moderation Department of your appearance?

1 Timothy 2:9—

Proverbs 7:10—

Make a "Checklist for Moderation" drawn from the John MacArthur article "What's a Woman to Wear?"

As you consider God's description of the godly "older women" in Titus 2:3, where do you see modesty, propriety, and moderation fitting in?

Note: The woman who is "reverent in behavior" is a woman who has a keen awareness that she is living her life in the presence of God. How do you think such a cultivated awareness would make a difference in a woman's appearance?

So…what's a woman to wear? Are you using this checklist for your daily grooming? And how would doing so make a difference? (And don't fail to share this biblical checklist with your daughters!) Check yourself…

> …for modesty—"Do I look pure?" "Am I wearing too little?"

> …for propriety—"Is my appearance reflecting a proper image of a woman of God?"

> …for moderation—"Would my appearance cause someone to stumble?" "Am I wearing too much?"

> …for wisdom—The wise woman will pass this test!

Practical Beauty Tips

✓ Dress up—Esther was "Queen Esther"! As you read Esther 5:1-2, how was she appropriately and properly attired for her status as queen and for the nature of her business (see Esther 4:8) as she stood before her husband, the king?

The Proverbs 31 woman was a fabric merchant (Proverbs 31:24) and an artisan. How was her clothing appropriate and proper for her status (verse 22)?

How do the examples of these two wise and godly women—Esther and the Proverbs 31 woman—guide you in your dressing up…versus today's current tendency to dress down?

✓ Fix up—How do these scriptures encourage you to think of others, even in the matter of your appearance?

Romans 12:10—

Philippians 2:3-4—

✓ Clean up—How does Proverbs 27:9 speak of the results of our efforts to clean up and spruce up a little?

✓ Look up—Beloved, you and I simply must pray about everything…even about what we wear, especially as we learn how important our clothing and appearance is as women who represent God. What kind of heart is it that looks up, that is concerned with God's standard and God's approval?

1 Peter 3:4—

1 Peter 3:15—(P.S.—To *sanctify* means to enshrine, to love, to obey, and to set apart as a priority.)

Just for Today

🌹 *Just for today…*

🌹 *Just for tomorrow…*

🌣 *Just for this week…*

—Seeking a Heart of Wisdom—

Please read the "Seeking a Heart of Wisdom" section in your book again. As you consider the contents of this chapter and God's wisdom for your life as a woman, what one timeless principle or truth spoke to your heart…and what do you plan to do about it?

I Need Help with...
My Appetite

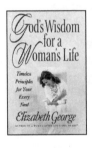

In your personal copy of *God's Wisdom for a Woman's Life* read the chapter titled "I Need Help with...My Appetite." Make notes here about what from this chapter meant the most to you or offered you the greatest challenge or helped you grow in wisdom.

The Bible has a lot to say about different kinds of appetites, about our many desires. Many of these desires are for the wrong things. But wisdom from the Bible helps us keep our desires in check and under control, as well as guiding us to choose the right things. There are many appetites that we could discuss, appetites such as materialism, the craving of worldly things, and sensual lusts that affect our shopping and reading and viewing habits. But for this lesson we'll limit our study of appetites and focus on just one aspect of appetite—food.

Better Eating…God's Way

To get a serious perspective on our eating habits, begin by copying out 1 Corinthians 10:31 from your version of the Bible. Then write out *Rule #1* for better eating God's way.

Rule #1—

First, the physical—Have you ever tried to start up your car and in the process flooded the engine with too much gas? Well, that's what happens when we "flood" our body with too much food at one time. God created us, and He knows what's best, whether that best is in the spiritual realm or in the physical. That's why knowing and paying attention to His guidelines regarding food is vitally important.

From the very beginning of the Bible, God has been most interested in what His children eat and do not eat. For instance, in the fewest words possible, what instructions were given to the following people?

Adam and Eve in Genesis 2:16-17—

The Israelites in Leviticus 11:1-2—

As a note, in giving such instructions God was protecting His people through dietary and hygienic restrictions. But, more importantly, He was stressing obedience to Him and the separation of His people from idolatrous nations.[17]

God is also most interested in how much His children eat. What are a few of His guidelines, and what happens when we ignore them?

Proverbs 23:20-21—

Proverbs 25:16—

Everyone has overeaten at some time! Describe such a time for you and its physical effects. In other words, how did you feel?

Next, the financial—Revisit Proverbs 23:20-21. What does it say will happen in the Financial Department to the one who drinks and eats too much?

Now, an exercise—Look back over this past week. How much money did you and your family spend on food?

Then go a step further: How much money did you spend on eating out and bringing home fast foods?

What does this reveal about your family's eating habits?

What does this reveal about your family's financial habits?

List several ways you can make food a less costly item in your family budget.

—

—

And, of course, the spiritual—This lesson is about appetite, physical appetite. Where can a Christian go for help with an eating problem according to...

...Galatians 5:16?

...Galatians 5:22-23?

Also what spiritual help does Romans 13:14 give regarding any and all appetites?

Bonus question—What practical help does Romans 13:14 give you about such issues as what you put on your grocery list, purchase at the store, bring home, place in the cupboard and pantry, and make readily available for your moments of weakness? (In other words, are you planning ahead and providing for sinful gratification? Are you planning to overindulge ahead of time?)

Daniel was a man in the Bible who showed a heart for obeying God in the area of food. Map out the scenes and the order of events in…

…Daniel 1:3-5

…Daniel 1:8-14

…Daniel 1:15-16

Read again the quote by Elisabeth Elliot on the facing page of this chapter in your book. How do you think greater discipline in the area of food can strengthen your "spiritual fiber"?

The seven deadly sins, according to St. Thomas Aquinas, are:

envy	sloth
greed	pride
lust	anger

gluttony

Another exercise—Look back over this past week. How much time did you and your family spend purchasing, preparing, and eating snack foods (...and wearing a path in the carpet as you traipsed back and forth to the refrigerator before and after meals)? Shine the spotlight on your habits and patterns. Look for the excesses and practices that indicate a lack of control. (Remember, bad habits are like a comfortable bed...easy to get into, but hard to get out of!)

A Prayer for Wisdom

Lord, may a lifestyle of physical fatigue, financial folly, spiritual deadening, and the practical misuse of my time not be true of me. Help me be a woman who yearns to live my life in a wise way—in Your way!

Are the words of this prayer the words of your heart? I know they are for me! Pray them now...and every day...until the wisdom taught in God's Word about food is yours. Then you will be a woman who walks in wisdom!

Just for Today

❧ *Just for today...*

❧ *Just for tomorrow...*

❧ *Just for this week...*

Seeking a Heart of Wisdom

Please read the "Seeking a Heart of Wisdom" section in your book again. As you consider the contents of this chapter and God's wisdom for your life as a woman, what one timeless principle or truth spoke to your heart…and what do you plan to do about it?

16

I Need More Help with...
My Appetite

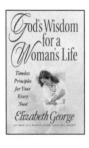

In your personal copy of *God's Wisdom for a Woman's Life* read the chapter titled "I Need More Help with...My Appetite." Make notes here about what from this chapter meant the most to you or offered you the greatest challenge or helped you grow in wisdom.

Better Eating...God's Way!

As we begin this lesson, copy out *Rule #1* from the previous lesson. Then, as you work your way through the remaining rules for better eating God's way, record each rule.

Rule #1—

Rule #2—

Read Proverbs 30:8-9, a guiding principle for every wise woman's life! How do these verses define moderation in food for you?

What is the danger of too much?

And what is the danger of too little?

According to the New Testament, what are the basics of life (1 Timothy 6:6-8)?

Verse 6—

Verse 8—

Where are you on the Contentment Scale? Are you overly concerned about food...or are you content with just enough (see Proverbs 30:8)? Please explain your answer.

Bonus question—What is one physical effect of eating more than just enough?

Unless you are in the percentage of the world's people who are deprived of the basics of living, you have much to be thankful for. Why not pause and offer up a prayer of thanksgiving to the Lord now?

Rule #3—

Copy Proverbs 25:16 here. Then put it in your own words.

Look again at the story of Eve in Genesis 3:1-6. Then read Genesis 2:16. How did Eve choose her own way regarding eating and thus violate *Rule #3?*

What lessons can we learn from Eve about trusting God for our daily bread?

Rule #4—

Addictions are a terrible thing, aren't they? Alcohol. Tobacco. Drugs. And yes, food! It's a fact—when we come to the table and can't control our eating habits, then we must face the truth: We have a problem with food!

Begin now by writing out Paul's words of wisdom in 1 Corinthians 6:12 here.

Think a minute. Are there any appetites that are mastering you? And what steps can you take to overcome them so that Paul's battle cry applies to your life too?

And what great resource is available to you according to 2 Corinthians 12:9?

Rule #5—

Beloved, we have now come full circle. We started with 1 Corinthians 10:31 in our last lesson, and I want us to end with that same pivotal verse here. So...won't you write it out again?

Here in this lesson, our last two questions related to the steps you could take to overcome your appetites and addictions. How would this verse help?

Better Living...God's Way

I'm sure you agree that there is more to life than food! And that's the subject of this final section of your lesson. So...let's move beyond mastering our appetite for food and focus on the greater challenge—that of mastering *every* appetite!

As was noted in the previous lesson regarding God's servant Daniel, the matter of food was only Step 1 in God's preparation of him as a man whose spiritual fiber would be rigorously tested later on. Indeed, Daniel's life (as is everyone's!) was one rigorous trial after another. How do these scriptures point you to a way of life, to a life that goes beyond food to master the "all things" and the "anythings" and the "everythings" of life? (And yes, there are a few repeats, but repetition is a biblical way of teaching and learning—see 2 Peter 1:13.)

1 Corinthians 6:12—

1 Corinthians 6:19-20—

1 Corinthians 9:27—

1 Corinthians 10:23—

1 Corinthians 10:31—

As you thread the teachings of these scriptures together, share...

> ...how you are more motivated to run the race for the prize of the upward call of God in Christ Jesus (Philippians 3:14).

> ...how you are more prepared to run the race.

> ...how you are more informed to run the race.

Now, dear friend, what is the first thing you feel you must gain control over so that you can better run the race of your life?

Just for Today

🌹 *Just for today...*

𝔷 *Just for tomorrow…*

𝔷 *Just for this week…*

⟋ *Seeking a Heart of Wisdom* ⟍

Please read the "Seeking a Heart of Wisdom" section
in your book again. As you consider the contents of
this chapter and God's wisdom for your life as a
woman, what one timeless principle or truth spoke
to your heart…and what do you plan to do about it?

I Need Help with...
Discipline

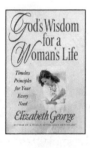

In your personal copy of *God's Wisdom for a Woman's Life* read the chapter titled "I Need Help with...Discipline." Make notes here about what from this chapter meant the most to you or offered you the greatest challenge or helped you grow in wisdom.

God's Wisdom Regarding Discipline

Recognize that discipline is a spiritual issue—Read the entire list of the fruit of the Spirit in Galatians 5:22-23. How important is self-control to the other fruit mentioned in these verses?

Readily acknowledge sin—We are told many times in the Bible to "walk" in a particular manner. What do these verses (and keep in mind that there are many others!) say about your walk?

Galatians 5:16—   Ephesians 5:15—

Ephesians 4:1—   Colossians 4:5—

Ephesians 5:2—   1 John 1:7—

Ephesians 5:8—   3 John 4—

Key in now on Galatians 5:16. How does walking in the Spirit help in the battle against the flesh?

Now describe the battle waged by every believer between the flesh and the Spirit as detailed in Galatians 5:17.

Write out these verses to get a better picture of the full effects and consequences of sin when it comes to the ministry of the Holy Spirit in your life.

Ephesians 4:30—

1 Thessalonians 5:19—

How do these two scriptures and situations impress upon you the importance and the way to keep a clean slate with God?

David shows us how—What did David look for as a result of his confession of his sins (Psalm 51:12)?

What desire and fruit followed David's confession and forgiveness (Psalm 51:13)?

Realize that discipline is an act of the will—How did Paul willfully deal with discipline in his life (1 Corinthians 9:27)?

Once again, how can you willfully deal with discipline in your life according to...

...Romans 13:14?

...1 Corinthians 6:12?

...1 Corinthians 9:25?

...1 Corinthians 9:27?

...Colossians 3:5?

...1 Thessalonians 4:3?

...2 Timothy 2:22?

...1 Peter 2:11?

The list of instructions, commands, and exhortations from the Bible regarding disciplined living truly goes on and on! Indeed, God is faithful to tell His children exactly what they are to do and not do. And it is our obedience to God that births, builds, and strengthens discipline. Now, the question is, Are you faithful to follow through, carry out, and obey God's wisdom? For instance, what area(s) of personal discipline are you now working to improve? And what specifically are you willfully doing to deal with it?

Rejoice with each victory—I don't know about you, but I battle with my flesh every day (and even every minute!) of my life. And I'm sure you can identify with Paul in his struggle. Read Romans 7:13-25 and briefly relate how Paul describes the battle every believer is fighting against his or her flesh.

Now that you are more aware of the struggle, what hope of victory does Paul give in Romans 8:1-2?

And what is your assurance of victory (1 John 5:4)?

Once again, who has victory (1 John 5:5)?

Remember that discipline mirrors maturity—As was stated in your book, each step of self-control and self-discipline leads to greater spiritual strength and maturity. As a result of victory in our Lord Jesus Christ (1 Corinthians 15:57), what resolves should you now have (1 Corinthians 15:58)?

—

—

—

What ability comes with maturity according to Hebrews 5:14?

Again, in verse 14, what activity makes this ability possible?

What can you do today "by reason of use"—or constant use and practice or habit—to develop and train yourself and your senses (sight, sound, touch, and so forth) to discern in your daily life what is right and wrong?

God's Wisdom Requires Discipline

Meet Eve—We've already looked at the sad tale of Eve's lack of discipline in Genesis 3. But please re-read verses 1-7 and fill in the spaces with the corresponding verses.

Eve talked too much, verse_____

Eve held back too little, verse_____

Eve wanted too much, verse_____

Eve ate too much, verse_____

Knowing what you've now learned in your study of wisdom, if you had been in Eve's position, how would (Lord willing!) you have handled the situation differently?

Now Meet Abigail—First, scan 1 Samuel 25 in your own Bible. Then list the steps of wisdom you observe Abigail taking in her difficult situation. What lessons can the wisdom of Abigail teach you about your life situation?

Just for Today

- *Just for today…*

- *Just for tomorrow…*

- *Just for this week…*

Seeking a Heart of Wisdom

Please read the "Seeking a Heart of Wisdom" section in your book again. As you consider the contents of this chapter and God's wisdom for your life as a woman, what one timeless principle or truth spoke to your heart...and what do you plan to do about it?

I Need Help with...
Diligence

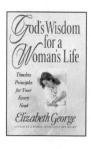

In your personal copy of *God's Wisdom for a Woman's Life* read the chapter titled "I Need Help with...Diligence." Make notes here about what from this chapter meant the most to you or offered you the greatest challenge or helped you grow in wisdom.

As you approach this next exercise, keep these instructions in mind for each scripture:

— The most important thing is to read the verses in your Bible. Remember, the Word of the Lord makes the simple wise (Psalm 19:7)!

— State how you can become diligent or more diligent in each area.

God's Wisdom Regarding Diligence

✓ Diligence affects your finances—"He who deals with a slack hand becomes poor, but the hand of the diligent makes one rich" (Proverbs 10:4).

✓ Diligence affects your livelihood—"He who tills his land will be satisfied with bread, but he who follows frivolity is devoid of understanding" (Proverbs 12:11).

✓ Diligence affects your income and productivity—"In all labor there is profit, but idle chatter leads only to poverty" (Proverbs 14:23).

✓ Diligence affects your contribution to society—"He who is slothful in his work is a brother to him who is a great destroyer" (Proverbs 18:9).

✓ Diligence affects your outcome—"Be diligent to know the state of your flocks, and attend to your herds; for riches are not forever" (Proverbs 27:23-24).

✓ Diligence affects your comfort—"He who tills his land will have plenty of bread, but he who follows frivolity will have poverty enough!" (Proverbs 28:19).

✓ Diligence affects your household (Proverbs 31:10-31)— The wise woman...

> ...rises while it is yet night (verse 15),

> ...girds herself with strength (verse 17),

> ...strengthens her arms (verse 17),

> ...works into the night (verse 18), and

> ...does not eat the bread of idleness (verse 27).

Therefore...

> ...her husband has no lack of gain (verse 11),

> ...she provides food for her household (verse 15),

> ...she makes tapestries for her home (verse 22), and

> ...her clothing is fine linen and purple (verse 22).

And then comes the reward from...

> ...her children rise up and call her blessed (verse 28),

> ...her husband also, and he praises her: "Many daughters have done well, but you excel them all" (verse 28).

Now look back at this remarkable woman's diligence and check the areas where you can become diligent or more diligent in your household. Then make notes detailing how you plan to get started.

Several Motivators for Diligence

Awareness of the brevity of life—What are the Bible's remarks on the brevity of life in the following scriptures?

1 Chronicles 29:15—

Job 7:6-7—

Psalm 39:4-5—

James 4:14—

1 Peter 1:24—

Whether we acknowledge the brevity of life or not, we have a choice. We can either follow the negative models of...

...Proverbs 6:10

...Proverbs 20:4

...Proverbs 21:25

or we can follow the positive models of...

...Proverbs 22:29

...Proverbs 31:13

...Proverbs 31:15

...Proverbs 31:16

...Proverbs 31:17

...Proverbs 31:18

.. Proverbs 31:19

...Proverbs 31:21

Now...what will your choice be? And while you're answering this question, list three things you'll do to get started right away.

—

—

—

Awareness of the purpose of life—Leaf through chapter 3 in your book, the chapter on "Purpose." As a quick refresher on purpose, the great energizer, what do the following verses remind you about God's purpose for your life?

Ephesians 2:10—

1 Corinthians 10:31—

Awareness of stewardship—How do these scriptures motivate you
  to be diligent about your stewardship?

Matthew 25:23—

Luke 12:42-44—

1 Corinthians 4:2—

2 Corinthians 5:10—

Awareness of time—First read Ephesians 5:15-16. Then analyze
  your average day. When do your peaks and valleys normally
  occur? Are they fairly consistent each day...or do things
  come up that alter a predictable pattern (things like late-
  night engagements, sick children who need care through
  the night)? Hopefully these altered plans are not the norm.
  Once you are aware of your highs and lows of energy, write
  below the times they occur. Then assign appropriate tasks
  for each period for tomorrow or this next week:

Time of high energy level _____

Activities for this period of my day:

  —

  —

  —

Times of low energy level _____

Activities for this period of my day:

—

—

—

Don't forget to evaluate your productivity at the end of the day and the week as a result of seeking to work more wisely with your time.

An Example of Diligence

Take a few minutes and scan chapter 2 of the book of Ruth and jot down what you observe of Ruth's diligence and what impresses you most. As we noted, Ruth is "an example of diligence." Now list two ways you can follow in her footsteps.

Just for Today

➣ *Just for today...*

❧ *Just for tomorrow…*

❧ *Just for this week…*

Seeking a Heart of Wisdom

Please read the "Seeking a Heart of Wisdom" section in your book again. As you consider the contents of this chapter and God's wisdom for your life as a woman, what one timeless principle or truth spoke to your heart…and what do you plan to do about it?

Seeking a Life of Wisdom

My dear and precious sister, reading companion, and fellow seeker of wisdom, we've come to the end of our sincere search for wisdom for many of the areas of our lives as God's women. My hearty congratulations to you! As I look back at what we've accomplished together, I'm greatly amazed! It's been lengthy in content, loaded with Scripture, and leveled at some serious issues in our daily lives.

But now I ask one more thing of you (and me, too!). I'm a great fan of "take-away truth." We've worked long and hard to find God's truth. And we've learned much about wisdom. Plus we've spent a lot of time—our precious, God-given time—seeking God's wisdom. We can't just let that time and God's truth pass away without noting what we've gained that is life-changing. So...

Look at the table of contents in the front of the book for a summary of the life-topics we've covered in our study. Then write out the three top timeless principles and life-changing practices you are positively taking away as "God's Wisdom for *Your* Life."

—

—

—

May God richly bless you as you walk in wisdom and follow His ways!

Notes

1. Donald S. Whitney, *Ten Questions to Diagnose Your Spiritual Health* (Colorado Springs: NavPress, 2001), p. 93.
2. Derek Kidner, *The Proverbs* (Downers Grove, IL: InterVarsity Press, 1973), p. 118.
3. Charles W. Turner, *Studies in Proverbs* (Grand Rapids, MI: Baker Book House, 1981), pp. 33-34.
4. Robert L. Alden, *Proverbs, A Commentary on an Ancient Book of Timeless Advice* (Grand Rapids, MI: Baker Book House, 1995), p. 32.
5. Louis Goldberg, *Wisdom for Living* (Chicago: The Moody Bible Institute, 1983), p. 44.
6. Leroy Eims, *Wisdom from Above for Living Here Below* (Wheaton, IL: Victor Books, 1981), p. 43.
7. The Tract League, Grand Rapids, MI 49544-1390.
8. Elizabeth George, *Life Management for Busy Women* (Eugene, OR: Harvest House Publishers, 2002), pp. 31-32.
9. Charles F. Pfeiffer and Everett F. Harrison, eds., *The Wycliffe Bible Commentary* (Chicago: Moody Press, 1973), p. 1446.
10. Mark Porter, *The Time of Your Life* (Wheaton, IL: Victor Books, 1983), p. 179.
11. Edward R. Dayton and Ted W. Engstrom, quoting Peter Drucker, *Strategy for Living* (Glendale, CA: G/L Publications, 1978), p. 179.
12. Benjamin R. DeJong, *Uncle Ben's Quotebook* (Grand Rapids, MI: Baker Book House, 1977), p. 199.
13. Elizabeth George, *A Woman After God's Own Heart* (Eugene, OR: Harvest House Publishers, 1997), pp. 169-170.
14. Eleanor L. Doan, *The Speaker's Sourcebook*, quoting Home Life (Grand Rapids, MI: Zondervan Publishing House, 1977), p. 50.
15. Kidner, *The Proverbs*, p. 148.
16. Doan, *The Speaker's Sourcebook*, quoting Jerry Fleishman, p. 23.
17. John MacArthur, *The MacArthur Study Bible* (Nashville: Word Publishing, 1997), p. 168.

Books by Elizabeth George

Beautiful in God's Eyes—The Treasures of the Proverbs 31 Woman
God's Wisdom for a Woman's Life
Life Management for Busy Women
Loving God with All Your Mind
Powerful Promises™ for Every Woman
The Remarkable Women of the Bible
A Woman After God's Own Heart®
A Woman After God's Own Heart® Deluxe Edition
A Woman After God's Own Heart® Audiobook
A Woman After God's Own Heart® Prayer Journal
A Woman's High Calling
A Woman's Walk with God
A Young Woman After God's Own Heart

Growth & Study Guides

God's Wisdom for a Woman's Life Growth & Study Guide
Life Management for Busy Women Growth & Study Guide
Powerful Promises™ for Every Woman Growth & Study Guide
The Remarkable Women of the Bible Growth & Study Guide
A Woman After God's Own Heart® Growth & Study Guide
A Woman's High Calling Growth & Study Guide
A Woman's Walk with God Growth & Study Guide

A Woman After God's Own Heart® Bible Study Series

Walking in God's Promises—The Life of Sarah
Cultivating a Life of Character—Judges/Ruth
Becoming a Woman of Beauty & Strength—Esther
Discovering the Treasures of a Godly Woman—Proverbs 31
Nurturing a Heart of Humility—The Life of Mary
Experiencing God's Peace—Philippians
Pursuing Godliness—1 Timothy
Growing in Wisdom & Faith—James
Putting On a Gentle & Quiet Spirit—1 Peter

Children's Books

God's Wisdom for Little Boys—Character-Building Fun from Proverbs
(co-authored with Jim George)
God's Wisdom for Little Girls—Virtues & Fun from Proverbs 31